I0485345

Become smart with your money with these 201 quotes from Robert Kiyosaki

DEDICATION

This ebook is dedicated for you, my wonderful readers who invest your valuable time to read this book.

INTRODUCTION

Is there anyone else who can inspire people to improve their financial life in the way Robert Kiyosaki does it ? I don't think that someone else can replace Robert Kiyosaki when it comes to teach people to improve their personal finance. If you want to understand anything about money, the teacher and mentor you have to seek after is Robert Kiyosaki.

I can not say how his books, tapes and teachings have literary changed all my perpestive about money than any others teachers in the same field.

Robert Kiyosaki has given everything to us about his knowledge and we are grateful for his generosity and his enlightment.

Needless to say, everything in this book is adapted from all the teachings and writings of Robert Kiyosaki. These small passages are full of wisdom and intelligence about money, entrepreneurship, investing and personal growth. So you have here, great information that can truly make a difference in your life. What do have to do ? Read and read again this book and I am sure that you will not be the person you were before reading it.

DOTCHAMOU ZAKARI

1 '' In my opinion, the United States and many Western nations have a financial disaster coming, caused by our educational system's failure to adequately provide a realistic financial education program for students.'' Robert Kiyosaki

2 ''If you think mutual funds are going to be there for you, if you want to bet your life on the ups and downs of the stock market, that's your retirement you're betting on. What happens if the stock market goes up and then comes crashing down again when you're 85 years old? You have no control. I'm not saying mutual funds are bad. I'm just saying they're not safe and they're not smart, and I wouldn't bet my financial future on them." Robert Kiyosaki

3 "Our schools are training people to be employees, to work for the rich. The second thing Idon't like about school is how they label a kid as smart or stupid at an early age. The reason I'm sensitive about that is because I was labeled stupid right from the start!" Robert Kiyosaki

4"If you look at the CASHFLOW Quadrant, you have the E, S, B, & I quadrants. The people who go to school are on the E and S side. The S stands for specialist like a doctor or a lawyer, and the E's are employees. But doctors and lawyers pay the highest taxes, right?" Robert Kiyosaki

5"Right. My mother wanted me to be a doctor. If I had followed that advice, I'd be paying the highest tax possible. They make a lot of money, but they pay the highest percentage in taxes. So that's why this relates back to "go to school." Robert Kiyosaki

6"See, without financial education you have to get a job. What's tragic today with so many people losing their jobs is that they're going back to school to get another job, but they're now competing with their kids. That's insanity. So, we're not saying jobs are bad. We're just saying as entrepreneurs that our job is to create jobs. The government doesn't really create jobs. They need more entrepreneurs " Robert Kiyosaki

7"Financial security is more important than job security. E's and S's get punished for making mistakes,

or they lose their job. B's and I's get richer from their mistakes because they learn from their mistakes."
Robert Kiyosaki

8"Taxes. The harder you work for money, the more you will pay in taxes, right? " RobertKiyosaki

9"The big difference between E's and S's, and B's and I's, is that E's and S's focus on the income statement, and B's and I's focus on the asset column."
Robert Kiyosaki

10 "In the year 2000, one gold coin cost $300. This huge bag I'm holding is $300 inU.S. quarters. Today, in 2010, that same gold coin costs thousands of dollars to buy. So the reason people have to work so hard to keep up is because the value of our dollars is going down. The insanity of getting another job, paying more taxes, and working harder when... How many dollars did the Fed print in 2009? "Robert Kiyosaki

11"From August of 2008 through 2009, they created about 1.5 times more paper dollars than they printed in the previous 200 years."   And it isn't the coin that changed. People don't understand that it isn't the price going up. It's the value of the dollar falling. It's the currency that's changing. The can of Campbell's soup in the grocery store is the same can with the same contents from back in 1950 when it cost 15 cents. Today it's $1.95 or whatever it is. What's changed is the dollar's value, not the can of soup". Mike Maloney (Rich Dad Advisors)

12 "The rules have changed. In 1971 the U.S. dollar stopped being money and it... It became a currency. It became debt." Robert Kiyosaki

13"The way you increase your means is to acquire more assets—not houses or cars—but assets. The reason so many people struggle financially is that they have no financial education. They may be a good doctor or lawyer or accountant or rock star, but if they don't know the difference between assets and liabilities and they keep buying liabilities instead of assets." Robert Kiyosaki

14 "There are four major expenses that keep E's and S's poor. Number one is tax, and taxes are going to go up because the Fed is printing so much money all over the world.

Two is debt. People leave college with tons of debt, use credit-card debt to make ends meet, and then use debt to buy their house because they think it's an asset.

Three is inflation. Inflation goes up because, as taxes go up and prices go up, then inflation goes up.

And fourth is retirement. You must put something away for the day when you stop working.

Those are the four main reasons E's and S's, as a general rule, have to live below their means. But if you have financial education and live on the B-I side, you can increase your means by increasing cash-flowing assets." Robert Kiyosaki

15"I think it's absolutely criminal that our school system does not teach us much about money. And what they do teach us is to put your money in the bank which means you lose more money, and then talk to a financial planner who'll put you into mutual funds. That is not financial education. That is educating people to give more money to the rich." Robert Kiyosaki

16"for folks like my mom and dad, the World-War-II generation, the industrialized generation, it was very smart to save money. For our generation, the baby-boom generation, saving money could be the stupidest thing you can do because the system is stealing your wealth through the very thing you work for—money itself, which isn't really money anymore. " RobertKiyosaki

17"Everybody used to tell me my house had appreciated in value. Again, that's capital gains versus cash flow. And what people are finding out now that the real estate market has crashed and the value of homes has been sucked out... now people are upside down on their home, and they're finding out it's a liability because they still have to pay the bank on that mortgage." Robert Kiyosaki

18"The reason I'm in real estate is for one reason—debt—because one of the easiest assets to get debt on is real estate. But if you're going to use debt, you've got to be highly financially intelligent. Otherwise, if you're not intelligent, just keep calling your house an asset." Robert Kiyosaki

19 "there are four primary asset classes. **One is business.** As an entrepreneur you own a business. **Number two is real estate**, and we love rental properties that cash flow, real estate that puts money in our pocket every single month. **Number three is paper assets**: stocks, bonds, mutual funds, and savings. Most E's and S's are in paper assets today. **And number four is commodities**: gold, silver, other precious metals, oil, and gas." Robert Kiyosaki

20"Our real estate that we own is all basically financed with our tenants, so that's what I consider to be good debt. So when we get real estate, we get proper leverage, and it's paid by all the residents who live in all of our projects." Robert Kiyosaki

21 "Many people are worried today or think investing is risky because they invest for capital gains. They're hoping the stock price goes back up. They're hoping their home value goes back up. A smart investor doesn't really care. A smart investor wants both capital gains and cash flow." Robert Kiyosaki.

22 "People say that I like real estate. But I don't really like real estate. I just love debt because it's so easy to get a loan on real estate, right? " RobertKiyosaki

23"Go to a bank and the banker will sell you mutual funds. But ask them if they will loan you money to buy those mutual funds, and the answer is no. But if we go in and say we want to buy real estate, they'll ask us how much we want." Robert Kiyosaki

24"I'm not anti-bank, and I'm not anti-debt. I'm anti-lack of financial education because there's good debt, and there's bad debt." Robert Kiyosaki

25 "when markets go up, greed sets in. And greed makes people stupid." Robert Kiyosaki

26 "Any time you have no control over your money, or the return of your money, you're gambling." Robert Kiyosaki

27 "Education's a process. For example, I entered Navy Flight School in Pensacola, Florida. Two years later, I

popped out as a Marine helicopter-gunship pilot on my way to Vietnam. That educational process transitioned me from a guy who couldn't fly, to somebody who became one of the best pilots in the world. The same thing happens with education. When you go to school, the question is, "What do you come out as?" When you go through the process of education, do you come out an employee? Do you come out as a person who needs a paycheck? Do you come out as a person always looking for a job? A person working hard and paying excessive taxes? Most people go to school and they pop out as E's and S's. To come out as a B and I, you need financial education because financial education is also a process." Robert Kiyosaki

28"The only way for you to have a genuinely secure future is for you to take control of that future. "Robert Kiyosaki

29"If you think mutual funds are going to be there for you, if you want to bet your life on the ups and downs of the stock market, that's your retirement you're betting on. What happens if the stock market goes up and then comes crashing down again on. What happens if the stock market goes up and then comes crashing down again when you're 85 years old? You have no control. I'm not saying mutual funds are bad. I'm just saying they're not safe and they're not smart, and I wouldn't bet my financial future on them." Robert Kiyosaki

30"When I was a kid, my parents taught me the same formula for success that you probably learned: Go to school, study hard, and get good grades so you can get a secure, high-paying job with benefits—and your job will take care of you. But that's Industrial-Age thinking, and we're not in the Industrial Age anymore. Your job is not going to take care of you. The government will not take care of you. Nobody's going to take care of you. It's a new century, and the rules have changed."RobertKiyosaki

31"My parents believed in job security, company pensions, Social Security, and Medicare. These are all worn-out, obsolete ideas left over single company—an ideal so proudly championed by IBM in its heyday—is as from an age gone by. Today job security is a joke, and the very idea of lifetime employment with a anachronistic as a manual typewriter. "Robert Kiyosaki

32"Many thought their 401(k) retirement plans were safe. Hey, they were backed by blue-chip stocks and mutual funds, what could go wrong? As it turned out, everything blue-chip stocks and mutual funds, what could go wrong? As it turned out, everything could go wrong. The reason these once-sacred cows no longer give any milk is that they are all obsolete: pensions, job security, retirement security—it's all Industrial- Age thinking. We're in the Information Age now, and we need to use Information-"Age thinking. Robert Kiyosaki

33"The economy is not the issue. The issue is you." Robert Kiyosaki

34 "Moaning and groaning won't secure your future. Neither will blaming Wall Street, the big bankers, corporate America, or the government. If you want a solid future, you need to create it. You can take charge of your future only when you take control of your income source. You need your own business. Robert Kiyosaki

35"An asset is something that puts money in my pocket. A liability is something that takes money out of my pocket. That's really all you need to know. If you want to be rich or get out of the rat race, simply spend your life buying assets. If you want to be poor or middle class, spend your life buying liabilities. Robert Kiyosaki

36 "If money is not first in your head, it will not stick to your hands." Robert Kiyosaki

37 "most people work for everyone but themselves: for the owners of the company, for the government through taxes, and for the bank that owns their mortgage. Financial struggle is often the result of people working all their lives for others, to wind up with nothing at the end of their working days. The solution is to mind your own business. Start buying real assets, not liabilities or doodads as I call them in Cashflow 101. Robert Kiyosaki

38 "It is not so much how much money you make, but how much money you keep, how hard that money

works for you, and how many generations you keep it for." Robert Kiyosaki

39 "If what you've been counting on doesn't happen, what other financial options can you create? That is financial intelligence. It is not so much what happens, but how many different financial solutions you can think of to turn a lemon into millions. Financial intelligence is how creative you are in solving financial problems." Robert Kiyosaki

40"Simply put, a profession is what you do for others and a business is something you do for yourself " Robert Kiyosaki

41"Who is going to get richer in the long run? Someone who works all their lives trying to save a million dollars? Or someone who knows how to borrow a million dollars at 10 percent interest and also knows how to invest it and receive a 25 percent per year return on that borrowed million dollars?" Robert Kiyosaki

42"To whom would a banker rather lend money? Someone who works hard for money, or someone who knows how to borrow money and have that money safely and intelligently work hard for them." Robert Kiyosaki

43 "Who would you have to be and what would you have to know in order to call your banker and say, 'I want to borrow a million dollars.' Then have the banker say, 'I will have the papers ready for you to sign in twenty minutes." Robert Kiyosaki

44"The poor and middle class have a hard time getting rich because they try to use their own money to get rich. If you want to get rich, you need to know how to use other people's money to get rich…not your own." Robert Kiyosaki

45"The most important work in the world of money is cash flow. The second most important word is leverage. " RobertKiyosaki

46 "Why is it that a banker will gladly lend you money to speculate in real estate, but will hesitate to lend you money to speculate in the stock market?" Robert Kiyosaki

47 "If you had a choice of education, would you choose to go to school to learn how to work hard for money, or would you rather go to school to learn how to have money work hard for you?" Robert Kiyosaki

48 "Who has to be financially smarter with money? Someone who works hard for money or someone who has money work hard for him? "Robert Kiyosaki

49"The rich are richer simply because the use different forms of leverage and they use more of it. Financial leverage is the advantage the rich have over the poor and the middle class. Financial leverage is how the rich get richer quicker." Robert Kiyosaki

50"One of the main reasons the middle class and the poor work harder, work years longer, struggle to pay off debt and pay more in taxes is because they lack a very important form of leverage... and that is the leverage of financial education." Robert Kiyosaki

51"One of the main reasons the middle class and the poor work harder, work years longer, struggle to pay off debt and pay more in taxes is because they lack a very important form of leverage... and that is the leverage of financial education." Robert Kiyosaki

52 "If you want to be rich, you need to know the differences between good debt and bad debt; good

expenses and bad expenses; good income and bad income; and good liabilities and bad liabilities. Simply put, good debt is debt that puts money in your pocket every month, and bad debt is debt that takes money from your pocket every month." Robert Kiyosaki

53"more leveraged tools are being created today, tools such as computers, the Internet, and more to come. The humans who can adapt to use these tools of leverage are the humans who are getting ahead. The people who are not leaning to use more and more tools of leverage are falling behind financially or working harder and harder just to keep up." Robert Kiyosaki

54"People without leverage work for those with leverage." Robert Kiyosaki

55"Rather than utilize the financial leverage the rich use, the poor and middle class tend to use physical leverage to try and get ahead. Physical leverage is also known as hard work. The rich get richer primarily because they use the financial tools of leverage and the poor and middle class do not, at least not in the same way the rich use the same tools." Robert Kiyosaki

56"Other types of leverage are health, time, education, relationships, tools, and spare time." Robert Kiyosaki

57 "The rich keep adding more and more leverage, which is why they get richer and richer." Robert Kiyosaki

58 "A winning strategy must include losing." Robert Kiyosaki

59 "Losers are people who think that losing is bad. Losers cannot afford to lose and often avoid losing at all costs." Robert Kiyosaki

60 "Many losers bet only on sure things…such things such as job security, a steady paycheck, a guaranteed pension, and interest from a bank account. Losers keep losing and winners keep winning simple because winners know that losing is part of wining." Robert Kiyosaki

61"If you truly want to retire young and retire rich, the place to start is with your own realities Robert Kiyosaki."

62 "The rich think the opposite of the poor and middle class. The poor and middle class think that having a safe secure job is smart. The rich think building a business is smart and job security is risky." Robert Kiyosaki

63 "Learning to build a business is like learning anything else. If you work for job security, you will work hard for most of your life. If you work to build a business, you many work harder at the start but you will work less and less in the end and you'll probably make

ten to 100 to 1,000 times more money. So which one is smarter?" Robert Kiyosaki

64"You do not have to be rich or poor to be greedy or generous." Robert Kiyosaki

65"The easiest way to become rich is by being generous. Anytime I want to earn more money, all I have to do is ask myself how I can serve more people?" Robert Kiyosaki

66 "Most poor and middle class expect to receive pay raises the longer they work at a job. It is called seniority or tenure. Can you see how wanting more money for doing the same amount of work can be greedy. Or wanting to be paid overtime or wanting to be paid extra if the job the person does is outside the job description. In my world, if I want more money, I first need to do more and more for less and less money, for more and more people, then I become rich." Robert Kiyosaki

67"Henry Ford became one of the riches men in the world because he provided automobiles for more and more people for less and less cost." Robert Kiyosaki

68"A big business owner will do his or her best to build a system to serve as many people as possible. A B business owner uses a system to serve as many people as possible." Robert Kiyosaki

69 "In your family, what was the reality on the following subjects? Smart or risky:

1. Job security

2. Building a business

3. A big house

4. Apartment houses

5. Saving money

6. Investing money

7 The rich are greedy or generous " Robert Kiyosaki

70"If you want to get rich, don't ask for a raise. Instead of asking for a raise, begin to ask how you can serve more people. In fact, if you are serious about becoming rich, you don't really want a raise. If you get a raise you are working for the wrong kind of money." Robert Kiyosaki

71 "There are three different types of income:

a) Earned income: Earned income is you working for money. It is the income that comes in the form of a paycheck. It is also the type of income you ask for more of when you ask for a raise, bonus, overtime, commissions, and tips.

b) Portfolio income: Portfolio income is generally income from paper assets such as stocks, bonds, and mutual funds. A vast majority of all retirement accounts are counting on portfolio income in the future.

c) Passive income: Passive income is generally income from real estate or businesses. It can also be royalty income from patents or for use of your intellectual property such as songs, books, or other objects of intellectual value." Robert Kiyosaki

72 "Why Rich Dad Did Not like Earned Income

In rich dad's mind, the worst kind of income to work hard for was earned income. To him it was the worst for four main reasons:

a. It is the highest taxed income and it is the income with the fewest controls over how much you pay in taxes and when you pay your taxes.

b. You personally have to work for it and it takes up your valuable time.

c. There is very little leverage in earned income. The primary way most people increase their earned income is by working harder.

d. There is often no residual value for you work. In other words, you work, get paid, and then have to work again to be paid again. Again, to the rich there is very little leverage in working for earned income." Robert Kiyosaki

73 "Most people I knew dreamed of high-paying jobs with lots of earned income. Teaching people to spend their lives working for earned income is like teaching someone to be a high-paid slave for life." Robert Kiyosaki

74 "Why Rich Dad Liked Passive Income, Although he did receive all three types of income, if given the choice among the three, he would take passive income all the time. Why? Because it was the income he had to work the least for, it is often the least taxed, and it earned him some of the highest returns consistently over a long period of time. In other words, he worked hard for passive income because, in the long run, he worked less and less, served more and more people, and earned more and more the older he got." Robert Kiyosaki

75"50 Percent Money, Rich dad often called earned income, the income you receive from a paycheck, "50 percent money." The reason he called it 50 percent money was because no matter how much money you earned, the government always took at least 50 percent of it or more in one way or another. As most people know, you are taxed when you earn, spend, save, invest, and when you die. Rich dad had a difficult time understanding people who spent their lives in search of a higher paying job or a pay raise. He often said, "When you get a raise, so does the government." To him, spending your life working hard for 50 percent money was not the financially intelligent thing to do." Robert Kiyosaki

76"Today, the best way to earn more and work less is via owning your own business. It continues to be the best loophole in the world. One reason to start your own

business is the difference in when you pay your taxes."
Robert Kiyosaki

77 "The Problem with a 401(k)

Although I recommend that everyone have and maximize contributions to a 401(k), if they qualify for one, there is one major flaw I see in it. The flaw is that although you save your money in it and it hopefully grows free of the 20 percent capital gains tax when you withdraw it at retirement time, you are taxed at the 50 percent tax rate off earned income. Even though you believe you are investing in portfolio or 20 percent money, when you cash in, you are still taxed at earned income rates. That means you work all your life for 50 percent money, and when you retire you are still taxed at the 50 percent rate." Robert Kiyosaki

"The second problem with a 401(k) is that it only works for people who are planning on being poor. If your income remains high after you retire, you continue to pay higher taxes on your retirement money because your income went up, not down." Robert Kiyosaki

78"The problem with Social Security is that it only works for people who want to be poor. If after you retire and you find that Social Security is not enough for you to live on, and you go to work for earned income, the government will begin reducing your Social Security payments. In other words, the only way to receive a full payment is to choose to be poor, in most cases." Robert Kiyosaki

79"I teach, write and create board games. It's not for the money, although the money is good. There are far easier ways to make money. I teach and create educational products out of a deep concern. I believe our country is in trouble and so are millions of our people." Robert Kiyosaki

80"I believe we need to train more kids to be Bs, entrepreneurs who create jobs, and all kids to be investors in the I quadrant. Today, our schools do a pretty good job educating people to be Es or Ss, but hardly any education is allocated to be Bs or Is." Robert Kiyosaki

81"Instead of walking away with a solid financial education, most kids leave school- some already deeply in debt - prepared only to work hard, save money, get out ofdebt, invest for the long term and diversify." Robert Kiyosaki

82 "Today, our world faces some serious financial problems:

Some ofthe more pressing ones are:

a. Value ofthe dollar falling

b. National debt increasing

c. Baby boomers starting to retire

d. Oil prices rising

e. Gap increasing between the rich and everyone else

f. Wages decreasing

g. Jobs being exported

h. Social Security and Medicare going bankrupt

i. Savings being wiped out

j. Lack of financial education being taught" Robert Kiyosaki

83 "The pressing questions are:

a. What can we do?

b. What are the solutions to these problems?

c. Is our financial IQ high enough cosolve these problems?

d. How do we avoid becoming victims of these problems?

e. How do we protect our families from falling victim to these problems?" Robert Kiyosaki

84 "Rather than increasing the financial IQ of the population, we taught people to expect the government to solve their personal problems for them. This is why no politician dares touch Social Security and Medicare ... even though most ofus know these programs are doomed." Robert Kiyosaki

85"The reason why I write , speak and create educational games and other products is because I want people to become rich and solve their own financial problems rather than expect others to solve their problems for them. I agreed that by giving people money, I only made the problem bigger, harder to solve and more dangerous." Robert Kiyosaki

86 "Donald and I are concerned that most people do not choose to learn to manage their own money or learn to invest their own money. Instead of learn, they simply turn their money over to experts and then hope and pray their experts are truly experts." Robert Kiyosaki

87"Every generation will have its own unique set of financial problems. For my parents' generation, their challenges included a Depression and a World War. Their solution to those problems was to go to school, get a safe and secure job with benefits, retire at 65, and play golf for the rest of their lives." Robert Kiyosaki

88"For many of my parents' generation, a good education and a good job were adequate for financial survival." Robert Kiyosaki

89"My generation, the baby-boom generation, faces a set of different financial problems. Today, a good college education and a good job are not enough. To make matters worse, jobs are being exported overseas" Robert Kiyosaki

90 "Today, fewer and fewer companies have Defined Benefit Pension plans. Because Defined Benefit Pension plans are so expensive, companies that do have them are starting to alter them or discontinue them simply to save money. Companies do not want to pay for employees for life." Robert Kiyosaki

91"Donald Trump and I use debt to get richer. Our bankers love us. Our bankers want us to borrow as much money as we can because borrowers make them richer. This is called other people's money '' (OPM). Robert Kiyosaki

92"Donald and I recommend more financial education for you because we want you to be smarter when it comes to the use of debt. If we have more debtors, our nation's economy will grow.If we have more savers, our economy will shrink." Robert Kiyosaki

93"If you can understand that debt can be good, and carefully learn to Use debt as leverage, you will gain an advantage over most savers." Robert Kiyosaki

94"One of the differences between mutual funds and hedge funds is leverage. Hedge funds often use borrowed money. Why do they use borrowed money? With borrowed money, you can increase your ROI, your return on investment, if you are a smart investor. In other words, the more ofyour own money you use, the lower your returns." Robert Kiyosaki

95"I did not have a great education, nor was I born into a rich family. The one thing I did have was a rich dad who taught me to use my mind to make money … and not to make excuses. Rich dad hated excuses." Robert Kiyosaki

96 "Whenever I meet someone who is unhappy, unhealthy and unwealthy, I know it is simply because he or she has lost control of his or her mind, the greatest tool given to us by God." Robert Kiyosaki

97 "Although Donald and I have money today, we have both experienced financial losses. If we had used our minds to blame others or to make excuses, we would both be poor today." Robert Kiyosaki

98"A well-trained and disciplined investor can gain much higher returns with much less risk and less money, but it takes leverage ... and leverage requires you to educate yourself and to use your mind wisely." Robert Kiyosaki

99" In Vietnam, I gained a very strong faith in a Higher Power. There were many times I should have died or saw a friend who should have died, yet we miraculously escaped harm. In business, I have a strong faith that if I work with the highest good and fulfill a mission, a higher calling, I will enlist the powers of a supreme being. I believe that if I cheat, lie or I am not forthright, I diminish the power of what Native Americans refer to as the Great Spirit. I also believe the more I strive to work at the highest legal, ethical and moral standards, the more the power of the Great Spirit enters my business." Robert Kiyosaki

100 "Often, the more money you make the more money you spend; that's why more money doesn't make you rich – assets make you rich." - Robert Kiyosaki

101 "The most life destroying word of all is the word tomorrow." - Robert Kiyosaki

102 "The size of your success is measured by the strength of your desire; the size of your dream; and how you handle disappointment along the way." - Robert Kiyosaki

103 "I'd rather welcome change than cling to the past." - Robert Kiyosaki

104 "The most successful people are mavericks who aren't afraid to ask why, especially when everyone thinks it's obvious." - Robert Kiyosaki

105 "Hoping drains your energy. Action creates energy." - Robert Kiyosaki

106 "The more a person seeks security, the more that person gives up control over his life." - Robert Kiyosaki

107 "Everyone can tell you the risk. An entrepreneur can see the reward." - Robert Kiyosaki

108 "A plan is a bridge to your dreams. Your job is to make the plan or bridge real, so that your dreams will

become real. If all you do is stand on the side of the bank and dream of the other side, your dreams will forever be just dreams. - Robert Kiyosaki

109 "You'll often find that it's not mom or dad, husband or wife, or the kids that's stopping you. It's you. Get out of your own way." - Robert Kiyosaki

110 "The only difference between a rich person and poor person is how they use their time" - Robert Kiyosaki

111 "Your choices decide your fate. Take the time to make the right ones. If you make a mistake, that's fine; learn from it & don't make it again." - Robert Kiyosaki

112 "If you're the kind of person who has no guts, you just give up every time life pushes you. If you're that kind of person, you'll live all your life playing it safe, doing the

right things, saving yourself for something that never happens. Then, you die a boring old person." - Robert Kiyosaki

113 "Money is really just an idea." - Robert Kiyosaki

114 "Talk is cheap. Learn to listen with your eyes. Actions do speak louder than words. Watch what a person does more than what he says." - Robert Kiyosaki

115 "The moment you make passive income and portfolio income a part of your life, your life will change. Those words will become flesh." - Robert Kiyosaki

116 "If you realize that you're the problem, then you can change yourself, learn something and grow wiser. Don't blame other people for your problems." - Robert Kiyosaki

117 "As I said, I wish I could say it was easy. It wasn't, but it wasn't hard either. But without a strong reason or purpose, anything in life is hard. " - Robert Kiyosaki

118 "The single most powerful asset we all have is our mind. If it is trained well, it can create enormous wealth in what seems to be an instant." - Robert Kiyosaki

119 "Find the game where you can win, and then commit your life to playing it; and play to win." - Robert Kiyosaki

120 "The power of "can't": The word "can't" makes strong people weak, blinds people who can see, saddens happy people, turns brave people into cowards, robs a genius of their brilliance, causes rich people to think poorly,

and limits the achievements of that great person living inside us all." - Robert Kiyosaki

121 "One of the great things about being willing to try new things and make mistakes is that making mistakes keeps you humble. People who are humble learn more than people who are arrogant." - Robert Kiyosaki

122 "Intelligence solves problems and produces money. Money without financial intelligence is money soon gone." - Robert Kiyosaki

123 "Start small and dream big." - Robert Kiyosaki

124 "Emotions are what make us human. Make us real. The word 'emotion' stands for energy in motion. Be truthful about your emotions, and use your mind and emotions in your favor, not against yourself." –Robert Kiyosaki

125 "You're only poor if you give up. The most important thing is that you did something. Most people only talk and dream of getting rich. You've done something." - Robert Kiyosaki

126 "If you want to be financially-free, you need to become a different person than you are today and let go of whatever has held you back in the past." - Robert Kiyosaki

127 "The philosophy of the rich and the poor is this: the rich invest their money and spend what is left. The poor spend their money and invest what is left." - Robert Kiyosaki

128 "Sight is what you see with your eyes, vision is what you see with your mind." - Robert Kiyosaki

129 "In school we learn that mistakes are bad, and we are punished for making them. Yet, if you look at the way humans are designed to learn, we learn by making mistakes. We learn to walk by falling down. If we never fell down, we would never walk." - Robert Kiyosaki

130 "Never say you cannot afford something. That is a poor man's attitude. Ask HOW to afford it." - Robert Kiyosaki

131 "F.O.C.U.S – Follow One Course Until Successful" - Robert Kiyosaki

132 "Your future is created by what you do today, not tomorrow" - Robert Kiyosaki

133 "I find so many people struggling, often working harder, simply because they cling to old ideas. They want things to be the way they were; they resist change. Old ideas are their biggest liability. It is a liability simply because they fail to realize that while that idea or way of doing something was an asset yesterday, yesterday is gone."

- Robert Kiyosaki

134 "The more I risk being rejected, the better my chances are of being accepted." - Robert Kiyosaki

135 "One of the most stupid things to do is to pretend you are smart. When you pretend to be smart, you are at the height of stupidity."

- Robert Kiyosaki

136 "Find out where you are at, where you are going and build a plan to get there." - Robert Kiyosaki

137 "I am concerned that too many people are focused too much on money and not on their greatest wealth, which is their education. If people are prepared to be flexible, keep an open mind and learn, they will grow richer and richer through the changes. If they think money will solve the problems, I am afraid those people will have a rough ride."- Robert Kiyosaki

138 "Most people want everyone else in the world to change themselves. Let me tell you, it's easier to change yourself than everyone else." - Robert Kiyosaki

139 "People who dream small dreams continue to live as small people." - Robert Kiyosaki

140 "The richest people in the world build networks; everyone else is trained to look for work." - Robert Kiyosaki

141 "There are those who make things happen, there are those who watch things happen and there are those who say 'what happened?'" - Robert Kiyosaki

142 "Skills make you rich, not theories." - Robert Kiyosaki

143 "Losers quit when they fail. Winners fail until they succeed."

- Robert Kiyosaki

144 "When you come to the boundaries of what you know, it is time to make some mistakes." - Robert Kiyosaki

145 "People without financial knowledge, who take advice from financial experts are like lemmings simply following their leader. They race for the cliff and leap into the ocean of financial uncertainty, hoping to swim to the other side." - Robert Kiyosaki

146 "The ability to sell is the number one skill in business. If you cannot sell, don't bother thinking about becoming a business owner." - Robert Kiyosaki

147 "The trouble with school is they give you the answer, then they give you the exam. That's not life." - Robert Kiyosaki

148 "Complaining about your current position in life is worthless. Have a spine and do something about it instead." - Robert Kiyosaki

149 "The fear of being different prevents most people from seeking new ways to solve their problems." - Robert Kiyosaki

150 "Winners are not afraid of losing. But losers are. Failure is part of the process of success. People who avoid failure also avoid success." - Robert Kiyosaki

151 "Successful people ask questions. They seek new teachers. They're always learning." - Robert Kiyosaki

152 "If you want to be rich, you need to develop your vision. You must be standing on the edge of time gazing into the future." - Robert Kiyosaki

153 "If you're still doing what mommy and daddy said for you to do (go to school, get a job, and save money), you're losing." - Robert Kiyosaki

154 "Too many people are too lazy to think. Instead of learning something new, they think the same thought day in day out." - Robert Kiyosaki

155 "Education is cheap; experience is expensive." - Robert Kiyosaki

156 "There are no mistakes in life, just learning opportunities." - Robert Kiyosaki

157 "The love of money is not the root of all evil. The lack of money is the root of all evil." - Robert Kiyosaki

158 "We all have tremendous potential, and we all are blessed with gifts. Yet, the one thing that holds all of us back is some degree of self-doubt. It is not so much the lack of technical information that holds us back, but more the lack of self-confidence." - Robert Kiyosaki

159 "When you are forced to think, you expand your mental capacity. When you expand your mental capacity, your wealth increases." - Robert Kiyosaki

160 "Making mistakes isn't enough to become great. You must also admit the mistake, and then learn how to turn that mistake into an advantage." - Robert Kiyosaki

161 "In today's rapidly changing world, the people who are not taking risk are the risk takers." - Robert Kiyosaki

162 "Tomorrows only exist in the minds of dreamers and losers" - Robert Kiyosaki

163 "Excuses cost a dime and that's why the poor could afford a lot of it." - Robert Kiyosaki

164 "People need to wake up and realize that life doesn't wait foryou. If you want something, get up and go after it." - Robert Kiyosaki

165 "If you want to be rich, simply serve more people." - Robert Kiyosaki

166 "You're only poor if you give up. The most important thing is that you did something. Most people only talk and dream of getting rich. You've done something." - Robert Kiyosaki

167 "You will make some mistakes but, if you learn from those mistakes, those mistakes will become wisdom and wisdom is essential to becoming wealthy." - Robert Kiyosaki

168 "When people are lame, they love to blame." - Robert Kiyosaki

169 "Inside each of us is a David and a Goliath." - Robert Kiyosaki

170 "It is easy to stay the same but it is not easy to change. Most people choose to stay the same all their lives." - Robert Kiyosaki

171 "It does not take money to make money." - Robert Kiyosaki

172 "Face your fears and doubts, and new worlds will open to you." - Robert Kiyosaki

173 "A mistake is a signal that it is time to learn something new, something you didn't know before." - Robert Kiyosaki

174 "There are no bad business and investment opportunities, but there are bad entrepreneur and investors." - Robert Kiyosaki

175 "A winning strategy must include losing." - Robert Kiyosaki

176 "If you want to go somewhere, it is best to find someone who has already been there." - Robert Kiyosaki

177 "Success is a poor teacher. We learn the most about ourselves when we fail, so don't be afraid of failing. Failing is part of the process of success. You cannot have success without failure." - Robert Kiyosaki

178 "Business is like a wheel barrow. Nothing happens until you start pushing." - Robert Kiyosaki

179 "Starting a business is like jumping out of an airplane without a parachute. In mid air, the entrepreneur begins building a parachute and hopes it opens before hitting the ground." - Robert Kiyosaki

180 "Business and investing are team sports." - Robert Kiyosaki

181 "If you want to be rich the rule of thumb is to teach others how to be rich." – Robert Kiyosaki

182 "The hardest part of change is going through the unknown." - Robert Kiyosaki

183 "Financial struggle is often the direct result of people working all their lives for someone else." - Robert Kiyosaki

184 "Being an entrepreneur is simply going from one mistake to the next. You must have the fortitude to continue on." - Robert Kiyosaki

185 "The wealthy buy luxuries last, while the poor and middle-class tend to buy luxuries first. Why? Emotional discipline." - Robert Kiyosaki

186 To be a successful business owner and investor, you have to be emotionally neutral to winning and losing. Winning and losing are just part of the game." - Robert Kiyosaki

187 "The problem with having a job is that it gets in the way of getting rich." - Robert Kiyosaki

188 "When times are bad is when the real entrepreneurs emerge." - Robert Kiyosaki

189 "Sometimes you win, sometimes you learn." - Robert Kiyosaki

190 "You get one life. Live it in a way that it inspires someone." - Robert Kiyosaki

191 "The biggest challenge you have is to challenge your own self doubt and your laziness. It is your self doubt and your laziness that defines and limit who you are." - Robert Kiyosaki

192 "When I started my last business, I didn't receive a paycheck for 13 months. The average person can't handle that pressure."

- Robert Kiyosaki

193 "Getting rich begins with the right mindset, the right words and the right plan." - Robert Kiyosaki

194 "Sometimes, what is right for you at the beginning of your life is not the right thing for you at the end of your life." - Robert Kiyosaki

195 "Workers work hard enough to not be fired, and owners pay just enough so that workers won't quit." - Robert Kiyosaki

196 "And when a banker says to you, 'Your home is an asset,' they are not really lying to you. They're just not saying whose asset it really is. Your mortgage is the bank's asset and your liability" - Robert Kiyosaki

197 "In the early 1980s, I began teaching entrepreneurship and investing to adults as a hobby. One of the problems I ran into immediately was that most people who wanted to start businesses or invest with greater confidence lacked the basics of financial literacy. Robert Kiyosaki

198 "You can teach a child to memorize the word 'bicycle' but you cannot teach a child to ride one. A child needs to learn how to ride a bicycle by doing." Robert Kiyosaki

199 "CASHFLOW is a board game because investing and financial analysis are subjects that you cannot learn by reading." Robert Kiyosaki

200 "I have observed thousands of people learning to be investors by playing CASHFLOW, Investing 101 and 202. They learn by doing things I could never teach by writing or by lecturing, just as I could never teach you to ride a bicycle. The games teach in a few hours what my rich dad took 30 years guiding me to learn."

Robert Kiyosaki

201 "Whenever you get a paycheck, the first bill you pay is to yourself. Not the car payment. Not the mortgage or rent money. Pay yourself a decent bit of money, and then immediately put that money into a separate investment savings account. And don't touch it until you're ready to invest it in some other way."Robert Kiyosaki

"Many of the very rich became rich in their spare time. So, if you have a job because you have financial responsibilities, keep your job but make better use of your spare time. When your friends go to play golf or go fishing or watch sports on TV, you can be starting your part-time business." Robert Kiyosaki

www.ingramcontent.com/pod-product-compliance
Lightning Source LLC
Chambersburg PA
CBHW021920170526
45157CB00005B/2107